COLORING MANDALAS 3

For Confidence, Energy, and Purpose

SUSANNE F. FINCHER

SHAMBHALA
Boston & London
2013

Shambhala Publications, Inc.
Horticultural Hall
300 Massachusetts Avenue
Boston, Massachusetts 02115
www.shambhala.com

9 8 7 6 5 4 3 2 1

First Edition

Printed in Malaysia

♾ This edition is printed on acid-free paper that meets the
American National Standards Institute z39.48 Standard.

♻ Shambhala Publications makes every effort to print on recycled
paper. For more information please visit www.shambhala.com.

Distributed in the United States by Random House, Inc.,
and in Canada by Random House of Canada Ltd

Library of Congress Cataloging-in-Publication Data

Fincher, Susanne F., 1941–
Coloring mandalas 4: for confidence, energy, and purpose /
Susanne F. Fincher.
Pages   cm
ISBN 978-1-59030-903-2 (pbk.)
1. Mandala. 2. Coloring books. I. Title. II. Title: Coloring mandalas
four.
BL604.M36F5563 2013
203'.7—dc23
2012021936

Introduction

Being and Doing in the World

Driving the flat open roads of West Texas one summer day, I noticed that whether my car was stopped or speeding along the highway, I appeared to be at the center of a vast circular space covered with tough, dry grass and mesquite brush. My gaze traveled into the distance, where the horizon was like the edge of a dinner plate, marking the end of the earth in every direction. Feeling the urge for a better look, I pulled over, got out of the car, and made my way through the brush to a sandy patch nearby. I was alone. The sun burned down, unchallenged in its position at the center of a clear blue sky that held nothing back. The intense light forced my eyes into narrow slits. A breeze touched my face.

I slowly turned, surveying the empty land while the wind whipped my skirt. Occupying the center of the earth as my eyes told me I was, I felt a rush of grateful camaraderie with the sun. I was not alone after all. Suddenly inspired, I picked up a piece of white caliche stone and scraped a circle in the crusty sand on which I stood. Within the circle I felt secure, anchored, protected, like a little one wrapped in a snug blanket. Standing tall at the center of my circle, I felt kinship with the land, the sky, the sun. I had joined with the vast cosmic forces at play in this American grassland. Like many before me at such times, I had constructed a mandala to bring the moment into focus, manage the energy it stirred, and draw the event into my personal domain of experience.

Mandalas (Sanskrit for "sacred circles") have been carved, painted, danced, visualized, and constructed since ancient times by human beings the world over. They are circular forms containing lines, patterns, and colors. More than just forms, mandalas have been used in personal devotions throughout history and often symbolize a desire to mark or set aside a special time or place. The impulse to create a mandala can arise in unexpected places, as I discovered on that drive through West Texas. Making mandalas can help us to feel connected to ourselves and to the world. This book focuses on using mandalas as a way to claim our own truths and to find our way in the world.

The Meaning of Mandalas

Some ancient mandalas are simply circles with a dot in the center that may symbolize the sun in the sky. Others are circles enclosing a plain cross. The division of the circle into four may connote the four cardinal directions, the four seasons, or even the front, back, and sides of the human body. The number four is significant in mandalas of orientation and relates to knowing oneself and one's place: of *being*, one of the themes of this book.

Another variation of a mandala divided in four is the circle enclosing a swastika, an ancient four-armed design that suggests turning. The swastika may allude to the cycling of time as observed in the sun's apparent movements, the phases of the moon, or even the stages of life and death that mark the lives of human beings. In its suggested movement, a swastika is like a wheel; that is, the rim is kept in place and moved by radiating spokes from a still center. As Jill Purce notes, "All images which prescribe these movements are essentially mandalic, centering and ordering, because, on whatever level, the movement is echoing the cosmic movement of which it is symbolic."

Some consider the swastika, with its four arms and clearly defined center, as a figure encompassing five points. The number five is significant as a symbol of the human body. Two arms, two legs, and one head add up to five. Therefore, the swastika—and other mandalas based on the number five—can suggest a human body in motion, or *doing*, the second theme of this book.

Mandalas, however, are represented not only by simple shapes; through time they evolved for ritual purposes into intricate forms with complex imagery. This is evident in many cultures, including in Christian iconography and in Tibetan Buddhist art. Esther Harding, a Jungian analyst, describes the process:

> In Christian mandalas, Christ Triumphant appears in the centre, surrounded by the emblems or symbols of the four evangelists—the bull, the eagle, the lion, and the angel—representing the four manifestations or emanations of the divine power in his relation to man. . . . These are all conventionalized or

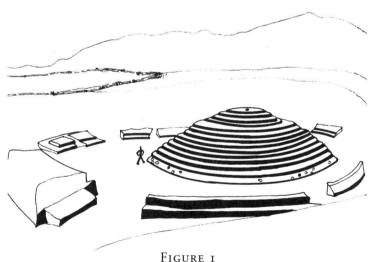

FIGURE I

Los Guachimontones is a ceremonial complex in the form of a mandala.

fixed ritual forms. Doubtless each originated in the vision of some person whose numinous experience presented itself in this guise, and gradually through the centuries, as one and then another found that his own experience could be expressed in a similar way, the original image underwent modification, until at last a definite form was crystallized out of the experience of the many and became established in the ritual as a sacred picture showing "the way things are."

The mandalas of Tibetan Buddhism have also been refined over centuries of use. They often consist of a blossoming of squares within circles within squares within circles peopled with many deities. These mandalas recall a worldview in which each man is a cosmic unit and the society in which he lives as well as its religious art reflect a map of the cosmos. Tibetan mandalas prescribe a visual journey through various layers and elements, moving from the periphery to the center. In this way, they are something like labyrinths. Their purpose, as Harding notes, is to "serve as an aid to visualization during meditation for 'building up' the individual mandala."

Mandalas can also be places of ritual in the form of structures or spaces that contain designs on flat surfaces. Among the earliest examples are Mesopotamian ziggurats, or stepped pyramids. These sites were tended by a priesthood that made detailed astronomical observations from their top levels. The movements of planets were charted to determine the dates of ceremonial occasions and to predict the future. A tree was often planted at the top of a ziggurat in honor of the goddess of the morning and evening stars (the planet Venus).

A recently discovered ceremonial complex in Mexico recalls the ancient pyramids of the Middle East. Los Guachimontones (c. 200–400 C.E.) lies west of Guadalajara (figure 1). The best-preserved structure is circular and stepped like a ziggurat, with sidewalks and rectangular platforms encircling it. These areas probably served as places for people to join in circle dances or to sit and observe ceremonial proceedings. On the top level of the circular structure is a hole that may have been used to anchor a pole. Perhaps a priest balanced atop the pole, taking the identity of a bird during ceremonies in honor of the wind god Ehecatl, revered by the local populace.

Various cultures ascribe different uses to mandalas. Labyrinths in Gothic cathedrals were built to replicate the pilgrimage to the holy city Jerusalem. Brilliant rose windows found in Christian churches capture and hold attention on revered beings depicted at their center as a method of religious instruction. Huichol Indians of northern Mexico create mandalas out of bright-colored yarn woven on crossed sticks. They call these "god's eyes" and believe that they provide a portal through which to see and be seen by god. Tibetan Buddhist monks create sand mandalas to invite gods, goddesses, and bodhisattvas to be present for sacred ceremonies. Navajo medicine men create mandalas of dry herbs, flowers, and powdered stones to reestablish cosmic harmony and bring about the healing of someone who is ill. All these mandalas reflect the urge to relate to the mysteries of human existence and to place oneself in harmony with natural forces in an effort to achieve peace, safety, and plenty.

Mandalas as Personal Expression

Mandalas are not limited to ancient civilizations. The desire to express oneself by drawing circles is apparently quite natural. Kindergartners create pure, simple mandalas that reflect their awareness of themselves and their surroundings. Mandalas come about in children's art at a particular developmental stage. Kids begin with random scribbles during infancy, and by about age three they are creating circles, suns, and crosses very similar to the art of ancient peoples. They go on to produce circles with the features of a human face and with lines suggesting arms and legs connected to the circle. Drawing mandalas may well support a young child's development of body image along with her discovery of herself as a unique being capable of willed action.

As we grow up, adults who create mandalas are perhaps unconsciously invoking their core identity in a process that is both retrospective and prospective, that is, looking within to the center point of self. They are thus scribing a new circle of self from which to witness, understand, and take action in the world. In geometry, drawing a circle is accomplished by establishing a single point, then scribing a line that is equidistant from the center along all its points. The center is literally a point of stillness around which the circle is drawn. Rudolf Arnheim, a perceptual psychologist, sees the centered circle as a fitting metaphor for the task of being human: "The spread of action from the generating core of the self."

Mandalas express human beings' ongoing dialogue between self and cosmos. In ancient times mandalas were created by individuals to both express and elicit a sense of harmony through synchronization with cosmic rhythms. In today's world both children and adults spontaneously create mandalas as a form of self-expression. Mandalas are also viewed in the West as reflections of psychological processes, as the Swiss psychiatrist Carl G. Jung proposed.

From his eclectic studies Jung deduced similarities in the psychological makeup of human beings. He formulated a concept of the psyche that explains these commonalities. According to Jung, the psyche includes both conscious and unconscious elements. He agreed with his contemporary the American psychologist William James that a person could not, at any given moment, be aware of the entire contents of the psyche. Consciousness, including personal identity, consists only of that which is "present to the thought at any time," as James wrote.

The center of consciousness is self-awareness, which Jung called *ego*. Information that is forgotten, not yet realized, or deeply embedded in the body's physicality Jung understood to be in the *personal unconscious*. He also posited a deep stratum of the psyche derived from shared human history that he dubbed the *collective unconscious*. The collective unconscious is the repository of natural ordering potentials accrued over thousands of years of human experience. Jung called these potentials *archetypes*. Human beings' shared inheritance of archetypes accounts for similarities such as the appearance of mandalas among diverse, widely separated populations.

Among the archetypes Jung discovered is one that functions as a natural centering and organizing principle for the whole psyche, even though it resides in the unconscious.

This center, known to Jung as the *Self*, to distinguish it from the ego, provides the matrix for development of the ego and motivates a desire for wholeness. According to Jung, the Self is the basis of an individual's personality throughout his or her life. The Self is also the generating force behind mandalas.

In a statement reminiscent of the Huichol beliefs about god's eyes, Jung said, "The mandala is indeed an 'eye,' the structure of which symbolizes the centre of order in the unconscious . . . looking into its own background" (see *The Archetypes of the Collective Unconscious*). Marie-Louise von Franz, a German-born Jungian analyst, comments on this remark, adding, "at the same time [the mandala] is also the Self, looking at *us*" (see *Projection and Recollection in Jungian Psychology*).

Jung found from his own experience as well as those of his patients that creating mandalas could help contain, process, and integrate information during psychological growth. He noted that creating mandalas provides a stabilizing anchor for individuals. Jung frequently saw mandalas in the artwork of his patients, and considered the appearance of mandalas as evidence that patients were changing in ways that expressed more fully their unique pattern of wholeness. The American art therapist Joan Kellogg applied Jung's ideas to her clinical experience. She incorporated the mandala designs Jung identified into her own theory of mandalas and personal growth, the Archetypal Stages of the Great Round of Mandala (hereafter referred to as the *Great Round*). Kellogg identified mandalas associated with twelve stages of human growth and development. Twelve is a number rich in historical, religious, and numerological meaning: twelve months of the year, twelve signs of the zodiac, twelve knights of King Arthur's Round Table, twelve apostles of Jesus, and twelve links of dependent arising in the Buddhist Wheel of Life. Twelve is made up of multiples of the numbers three (which is associated with dynamism) and four (linked to stability). A geometric figure with twelve sides, a dodecagon, is very much like a circle. For this reason, J. E. Cirlot concludes, "systems or patterns based upon the circle or the cycle tend to have twelve as the end-limit."

Kellogg arranged the stages and mandalas associated with her system in a circular configuration. The stages comprise a systematic progression toward the ultimate goal of wholeness. Each stage of the Great Round is characterized by a quality of consciousness, a view of reality, and particu-

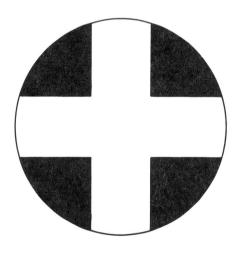

FIGURE 3
Mandala with a calm design.

FIGURE 2
Mandala representing Stage Seven of the Great Round: Squaring the Circle.

lar tasks, challenges, or concerns. Individuals are thought to repeat the cycle more than once as they grow and change through their lives. The twelve stages are called the Void, Bliss, Labyrinth/Spiral, Beginning, the Target, Paradoxical

Split/Dragon Fight, Squaring the Circle, Functioning in the World, Crystallization, Gates of Death, Fragmentation, and Transcendent Ecstasy.

In *Coloring Mandalas 4* we focus on mandalas of two stages of the Great Round: Stage Seven, Squaring the Circle, associated with *being*; and Stage Eight, Functioning in the World, where *doing* predominates. Stage Seven is a place of balance, integration, and self-realization. The term *squaring the circle* comes from a geometric conundrum that challenged ancient thinkers. Because the area of a circle is based on pi, whose absolute value cannot be determined, it is impossible to develop a square that has exactly the same area as a circle. The configuration of a square touching a circle suggests a link between the conceivable and the inconceivable (figure 2). The yoking of the known (ego) and the unknowable (Self) is the goal of psychological development according to Jung (see *Mandala Symbolism*). It is mediated by the mandala of Squaring the Circle and similar designs that indicate "the premonition of a centre of personality, a kind of central point within the psyche, to which everything is related, by which everything is arranged, and which is itself a source of energy. The energy of the central point is manifested in the almost irresistible compulsion and urge to become what one is."

These mandalas express a special experience of *being*.

FIGURE 4
Mandala representing Stage Eight of the Great Round: Functioning in the World.

They make a statement, and can be reminiscent of the designs of heraldic shields carried as the emblem of personal power. They are built on the structure of four within the circle. Jung was of the opinion that the number four signifies the harmonious juncture of two pairs of opposites, an auspicious indication of the resolution of inner conflicts. Some examples include Greek crosses, sun symbols like those in ancient mandalas, and squares inside or outside the mandala circle. Designs are usually symmetrical and convey centered stability, balance, and substance (figure 3). Coloring mandalas of Stage Seven, Squaring the Circle, may elicit the sense of calm self-assurance associated with this stage on the Great Round.

Stage Eight, Functioning in the World, is associated with action, energy, and *doing*. This is a time when you put your best effort toward accomplishing your goals. Stage Eight is associated with creativity, ingenuity, teamwork, and productivity. You are at your most effective during Stage Eight

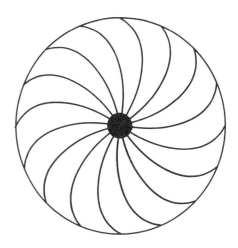

FIGURE 5
Mandala with a lively design.

on the Great Round, and your activities are valued in our culture. You often earn money for what you do while in Stage Eight.

The mandalas associated with Functioning in the World frequently display a structure based on the number five, which is a traditional metaphor for the natural body. Your head, arms, and legs stretch out to claim your body's five points of maximum extension in space. Your five-fingered hands allow you to take hold of and shape materials. Your five-toed feet support and balance your body so that you can move with confidence. Typical mandalas consist of five-pointed stars (figure 4), flowers with five petals, and centered swirls. Four-armed swastikas with a pronounced center providing the fifth element are also typical of Stage Eight.

The theme of *doing* associated with Stage Eight can also be found in mandalas that suggest movement with stimulating optical patterns. One of the gifts of human consciousness is the ability to imagine yourself in someone else's shoes. You experience this while watching a movie—when a character slips and falls, you flinch as if you were the one losing your balance. This is a form of empathy that also enables you to feel qualities of lines and patterns. Viewing a lively mandala design stimulates kinesthetic responses in your body (figure 5). When you add these kinesthetic responses to the physical movement you make when coloring mandalas, it is easy to see how you can become energized by coloring such designs.

Working with Mandalas

To get the most personal benefit from coloring the mandalas in this book, give some thought to the meaning of colors and forms you choose. Your mandalas reflect who you are at a given moment. They give you information about yourself expressed in the symbolic language of form and color. When you develop skills for deciphering the information in your mandalas, you are able to know yourself more fully. Your enhanced self-knowledge can provide a useful balance to your conscious-ego point of view. Information in mandalas can offer guidance from deep inner sources of natural wisdom and articulate realizations that can transform you into a person more nearly fulfilling your potentials.

One of the most direct avenues to interpreting your mandalas is through learning the meanings of the colors you use. There is no master list for the meanings of colors. Colors signify different things for each of us. They can have one meaning for us today and another meaning tomorrow. Here are a few simple steps to help you learn more about your colors.

Colors in Mandalas

Look in your closet at the colors of your wardrobe. An article of clothing you wear often and feel good wearing will be in a color you like. Something you have not worn in more than a year is probably in one of your less favorite colors. Translate this information to your choice of colors in your mandala. Those areas with a favorite color may represent parts of yourself you like or feel comfortable with. Less pleasing colors could represent less familiar or rejected aspects of yourself.

You can learn more about what colors mean to you by writing about them. I suggest you start a journal dedicated to your inner work with mandalas. In your journal, list all the colors you used in coloring your mandala. Write your answers to these questions about each one:

> How do I feel when I look at you?
> Do I like you? (If yes, why? If no, why not?)
> What do I remember about you from my childhood? (e.g., a color you were dressed in? the color of your room? a color worn by someone important to you?)

Read back through the answers to these questions and compile a list of your associations to each color.

In addition to your personal associations, another layer of meaning for colors arises from cultural usage. Role assignments linked to gender, race, and age mandate certain color choices. Liturgical or ceremonial uses of color may also be important for you. National and school affiliations, clubs, sports teams, and political parties may influence the significance of colors for you as well. Examine such personal meanings by writing about a color in your journal. Complete the sentence: In today's world you mean _____ (e.g., masculine, feminine, sports team, holidays, religious observances, etc.) to me.

After compiling information from your journaling

about colors, you will begin to know your own personal color vocabulary. This will help you decipher the significance of your choices when you color mandalas. Once you have mined your personal associations, you may want to explore some of the traditional meanings of colors.

You might ask, Now that I know what colors mean, won't I be less free when I choose colors for my mandalas? Perhaps a little, but this will not hamper the expression of your unconscious. For example, you may intentionally omit the color green from your mandala because it reminds you of a recent unpleasant encounter with a business rival. Your unconscious will simply express your uncomfortable feeling in another way. You will discover this when you do some journaling about the colors in your mandala. The hands don't lie, as my wise mentor in art therapy Lila Bonner Miller used to tell me.

When coloring, please remember that there are no right or wrong choices. The colors you select for your mandala will make it your very own. Color choices made by two individuals can result in versions of the same mandala design that look entirely different. You may choose colors you like for an enjoyable coloring experience. Using colors that are beautiful to you can be like listening to a favorite piece of music. Mandalas colored in harmony can be restful and refreshing. You may also experiment with using colors you dislike or never use. Intentionally picking out hues you usually pass over can be an effective way to bring into your mandalas, symbolically, parts of yourself that you overlook, dismiss, or reject. Growing toward wholeness requires that you acknowledge and accept some of your less admirable qualities along with the things you take pride in about yourself. Using colors you do not like can be a gentle and informative step toward accomplishing this inner work.

Forms in Mandalas

Learning your own personal meanings associated with shapes in the mandalas you color can give you additional useful information from your unconscious. To explore the meanings of forms, in your journal list each shape you see and free associate to it. That is, write down whatever you

think, feel, or remember as you look at the shape. After writing about all the forms in your mandala, read back through what you have written and identify a theme (or themes) that emerges. Write down the theme in a sentence or two. This is a message to you from your unconscious, inspired by the forms in the mandala.

Another approach to finding meaning in mandala forms could be the dialogue steps outlined in the section above, "Colors in Mandalas." Address the shape as an object. You might write something like, "Blue square, you are attracting my attention today. Tell me what message you have for me." Notice and write down the first words that come to mind, even though they may be surprising, impolite, or different from how you are feeling. Consider this information about you reliable, even though it may not fit with who you think you are.

Coloring vs. Creating Mandalas

A question worth asking is, does coloring mandalas have the same benefits as producing your own original mandalas? Certainly creating *and* coloring your mandala engage you more in the creative process. There is greater opportunity for your unconscious to express itself in the forms and colors you produce. However, when coloring the mandala designs in this book, you are bringing the mandalas to completion. The mandalas have open spaces that invite you to add your own touches. You can choose lines, textures, and media as well as colors. Essentially you are co-creating the mandalas.

Furthermore, the fact that you are attracted to mandalas enough to obtain this coloring book indicates that you are already attuned to mandalas. Verena Kast, a Swiss analyst, suggests that "people who feel drawn to [mandala courses] have an inner need to deal with mandalas." In other words, the centering power of the Self is activated, the relationship between ego and Self is highlighted at the moment, and personal growth is unfolding. The same can be said for an interest in coloring mandalas.

Regardless of whether you are creating mandalas or coloring predrawn mandala designs, you are held within the protective organizing power of the circle. Laurie, whose mandalas are included in my book *Creating Mandalas*, wrote: "I found that the circle itself offered a sense of safety that I had never felt. The boundaries of the mandala gave me a certain freedom to do whatever I wanted in the sacred center." Working within a circle is a powerful benefit of coloring mandalas.

During my workshops, I find that some people are uncomfortable creating a mandala from scratch. Anxiety constricts their self-expression. If you are a shy artist, the designs in this book can offer a more comfortable way to enjoy creative self-expression with mandalas. Perhaps you, like many people, fondly remember coloring as a child. This adult coloring book allows you to invite your inner child to share in a self-nurturing pleasure. Furthermore, the benefits of coloring mandalas are being confirmed by researchers. In one study by Nancy Curry and Tim Kasser, "[coloring] mandala designs drew participants into a meditative-like state that helped reduce their anxiety."

When coloring mandalas you interact with the form of the circle, which provides a safe container for self-expression. Your creative color choices are a significant contribution to completing the mandalas. In addition, color preferences reveal deeply embedded psychic contents and provide you with important messages from your unconscious. This, along with the personal meanings you discover in shapes within the mandalas, brings coloring mandalas ever closer to the "personal Rorschach," as Maralynn Slegelis calls it, provided by the experience of creating mandalas.

I'm No Artist

Sometimes you will encounter a voice of judgment when doing creative work. It usually says unhelpful things, like, "that looks stupid," "you can't do this," "you are no artist," "you should just give up now." Here are a few suggestions for managing this uninvited commentary from an inner critic:

Ignore it by focusing your attention on something else, such as your breathing or the sound your pencil makes on paper as you are coloring.

Say positive (equally true) things to yourself, such as, "there is no right or wrong way to do this," "I'm allowing myself to experiment with colors and just see what happens," or "I enjoy being creative."

Pause, take a few relaxing breaths, and address your inner critic: "That's your opinion. I appreciate the information. Now please keep silent while I enjoy this experience."

Say to your inner critic, "It's just a coloring book! Loosen up!"

How to Use This Book

Coloring the mandalas in this book will offer you an opportunity to express your nonverbal, curious, playful, courageous, and creative self. Approach coloring mandalas as serious fun. You might choose a design because it resonates with your feelings of the moment. You might select a mandala design that suggests something you would like to feel but do not feel right now. You might color a mandala as a gift for someone, in remembrance of a friend or family member, or in honor of an accomplishment you are proud of. You might take your coloring book with you for those times you are waiting in airports, during jury selection, or companioning loved ones in the hospital. Here is one woman's story:

During the time of my husband's in-hospital treatment for leukemia, I spent six to seven hours a day in his hospital room. While he didn't feel like having visitors, he had plenty of hospital staff in and out all day. I would pull back into a corner to make room for machines, people, and housekeeping. I felt insignificant and helpless in the face of this serious illness and the complex medical system that had taken over my husband's care. So I packed my mandala coloring book and my colored pencils and took them to his hospital room.

Coloring mandalas served me very well during those difficult days. It was one small way that I had complete control over something. When everything else felt well beyond my grasp, coloring mandalas was a comfort. Each day I chose a new mandala to color. I enjoyed the process of choosing colors and studying the forms of the design to decide what I wanted to highlight and what colors I wanted for each pattern. Before my eyes, a thing of beauty would emerge. I had a feeling of satisfaction and accomplishment.

In moments when the room was not busy, my husband and I chatted or he rested. I colored, and he enjoyed looking at the mandalas in progress and when completed. The mandala coloring book became a conversation starter for nurses, techs, and others who were curious about my industriousness. My sister, daughter, and sister-in-law picked up the book during their visits and colored mandalas of their choice. We borrowed techniques from one another such as shading, outlining, and blending colors. Our styles were unique to each person. Now the coloring book is like a nonverbal journal of that difficult time, reflecting back that there were moments of empowerment, beauty, and wholeness in spite of the difficulties inherent in facing a loved one's serious illness.

You can work straight through the mandalas in the book, or you may choose to work first on those you like best. One woman told me she selects a design that seems related to the dream she had the night before. Coloring the mandala is her way to honor the dream. Other approaches might be to select a mandala that gives you what you need at the moment. Perhaps you feel the need to relax, and choosing a symmetrical mandala design can be comforting. Or perhaps you are feeling frenetic. Coloring a mandala that matches your feelings can help you release energy so you can then relax and center. Conversely, if you have low energy and want to invigorate yourself, it might be helpful to color one of the mandalas you find pleasantly stimulating.

It is likely that you will not finish work on a mandala in one sitting. When you come back to it, I suggest you simply begin where you left off, making color choices that feel right in the present moment. Coloring mandalas at a regular time each day can become like a personal meditation. You might also like to share coloring with a friend by working together at the same time or taking turns coloring a mandala. For group sharing you could begin a mandala and then mail it to a friend. After her own creative additions to the mandala, she could send it to the next in your circle, and so on, until all have contributed. The finished mandala will reflect the essence of your group of friends.

I was told of another way to share coloring mandalas. A coloring book and pencils were donated to the library of a meditation center and were checked out by members to color. As the coloring book was returned and checked out again, more and more mandalas were filled in. Eventually the coloring book became an album of mandalas that members enjoyed leafing through for inspiration. Here is one last idea for coloring mandalas. A group on retreat tore out the blank mandalas from a coloring book and spread them on a table along with art supplies. Throughout the weekend, during breaks from separate activities, coloring mandalas gave teenagers and adults the rare opportunity to join together around the table and enjoy each other's company. As the weekend was coming to a close, all the mandalas were laid out to form a lovely collage that brought ceremonial closure to the bonding experience of the group's shared time together.

Suggested Materials

Media that work well for coloring the mandalas in this book are:

> Colored pencils (I recommend those a notch above student grade for satisfying results)
>
> Watercolor pencils (go over areas you have colored with a brush dipped in water to get the look of watercolor painting)
>
> Marker pens (these give a bold effect but can bleed through the paper, so place a paper towel underneath)
>
> Gel pens (especially good for highlights or small areas)

Try other media, too, if you like. Paper, yarn, or fabric collage, colored inks, crayons, even glitter can be used when you remove mandala pages from the book.

Coloring the mandalas in this book allows you to interact with forms that evoke both steady, centered *being* and active, skillful *doing*. Knowing the full measure of yourself and taking action from your centered being may be familiar to you. If so, coloring mandalas will be a pleasurable affirmation of who you are. If not, coloring the mandalas in this book can provide you with experiences that will expand your repertoire for *being and doing in the world*. May *Coloring Mandalas 4* spark many creative moments in your life.

References

Arnheim, Rudolf. *The Power of the Center*. Berkeley and Los Angeles: University of California Press, 1988.

Cirlot, Juan Eduardo. *A Dictionary of Symbols*. Trans. Jack Sage. New York: Philosophical Library, 1962.

Clark, Marilyn F. Personal communication with the author, 2011.

Cleary, Thomas. *I Ching Mandalas: A Program of Study for the Book of Changes*. Boston: Shambhala Publications, 1989.

Curry, Nancy A., and Tim Kasser. "Can Coloring Mandalas Reduce Anxiety?" *Art Therapy: Journal of the American Art Therapy Association* 22, no. 2 (2005): 81–85.

Fincher, Susanne F. *Creating Mandalas: For Insight, Healing, and Self-Expression*. Rev. ed. Boston: Shambhala Publications, 2010.

———. *The Mandala Workbook: A Creative Guide for Self-Exploration, Balance, and Well-Being*. Boston: Shambhala Publications, 2009.

Harding, M. Esther. *Psychic Energy*. 2nd ed. Princeton, N.J.: Princeton University Press, 1963.

Huang, Alfred. *Complete I Ching*. Rochester, Vt.: Inner Traditions International, 1998.

James, William. *The Varieties of Religious Experience: A Study of Human Nature*. London: Collier Macmillan Publishers, 1961.

Jung, Carl G. *The Archetypes of the Collective Unconscious*. 2nd ed. Trans. R. F. C. Hulla. Princeton, N.J.: Princeton University Press, 1969.

———. *Man and His Symbols*. Garden City, N.Y.: Doubleday, 1964.

———. *Mandala Symbolism*. Princeton, N.J.: Princeton University Press, 1973.

———. *Mysterium Coniunctionis: An Inquiry into the Separation and Synthesis of Psychic Opposites in Alchemy*. 2nd ed. Trans. R. F. C. Hull. Princeton, N.J.: Princeton University Press, 1970.

Kast, Verena. *The Dynamics of Symbols: Fundamentals of Jungian Psychotherapy*. Trans. Susan A. Schwarz. New York: Fromm International Publishing, 1992.

Kellogg, Joan. *Mandala: Path of Beauty*. Rev. ed. Belleair, Fla.: ATMA, 1984.

Leidy, Denise Patry, and Robert A. F. Thurman. *Mandala: The Architecture of Enlightenment*. New York: The Asia Society Galleries and Tibet House, 1997.

Purce, Jill. *The Mystic Spiral*. New York: Thames and Hudson, 1980.

Slegelis, Maralynn Hagood. "A Study of Jung's Mandala and Its Relationship to Art Psychotherapy." *The Arts in Psychotherapy* 14 (1987): 301–11.

von Franz, Marie-Louise. *Number and Time*. Trans. Andrea Dykes. Evanston, Ill.: Northwestern University Press, 1986.

———. *Projection and Recollection in Jungian Psychology*. Trans. William H. Kennedy. LaSalle, Ill.: Open Court Publishing, 1980.

Mandalas for Coloring

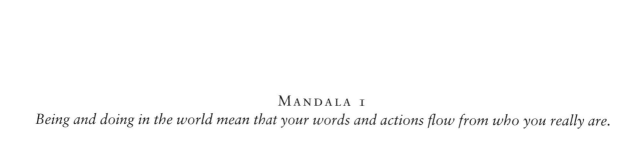

MANDALA 1
Being and doing in the world mean that your words and actions flow from who you really are.

MANDALA 2

This mandala resembles a Celtic shield embellished with jewels and knot work. Its center suggests a compass rose. The mandala communicates stability, protection, and clear thinking.

MANDALA 3

Intricate weaving suggests a soft square of knot work enclosing a Greek cross in the center space of this mandala. A strong sense of self can be expressed in gentle ways.

MANDALA 4

Rhythmic arcs recalling magnetic energy add a sense of dynamic movement to this mandala of strong, simple lines. Inner being gives rise to radiant doing.

MANDALA 5

Overlapping circles play in and around clear, lined squares: the convergence of being *and* doing.

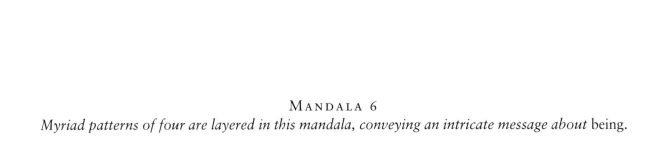

MANDALA 6
Myriad patterns of four are layered in this mandala, conveying an intricate message about being.

MANDALA 7

A tree symbolizes wholeness during a moment of self-reflection and cosmic connection.

MANDALA 9
This mandala is inspired by abstract tantric art of India. Which pathway to the center will your colors illuminate? There is no right or wrong way.

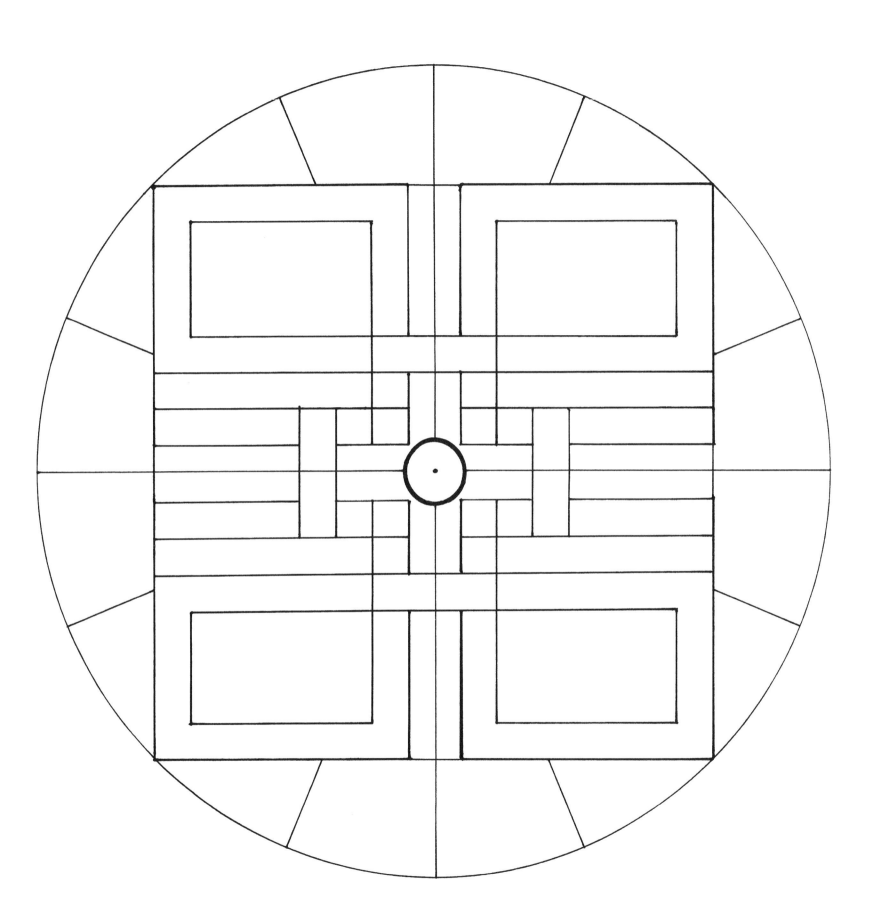

MANDALA 10

The centers of four overlapping rings are the corners of an interior square poised in readiness to move: the shift from being *to* doing.

MANDALA 11

The conundrum of Squaring the Circle is explored in this mandala with its rich array of lines and forms dancing in harmony.

MANDALA 12
Convivial abundance is suggested by the exotic flowers, large and small, that bloom in a lively balance within this mandala.

MANDALA 13
Flames illuminate the boundary of this mandala, suggesting the intensity of consciousness when being *is focused.*

MANDALA 14

Like a modern version of a jewel-encrusted Byzantine cross, this mandala holds multiplicity in one powerful design: a statement of being.

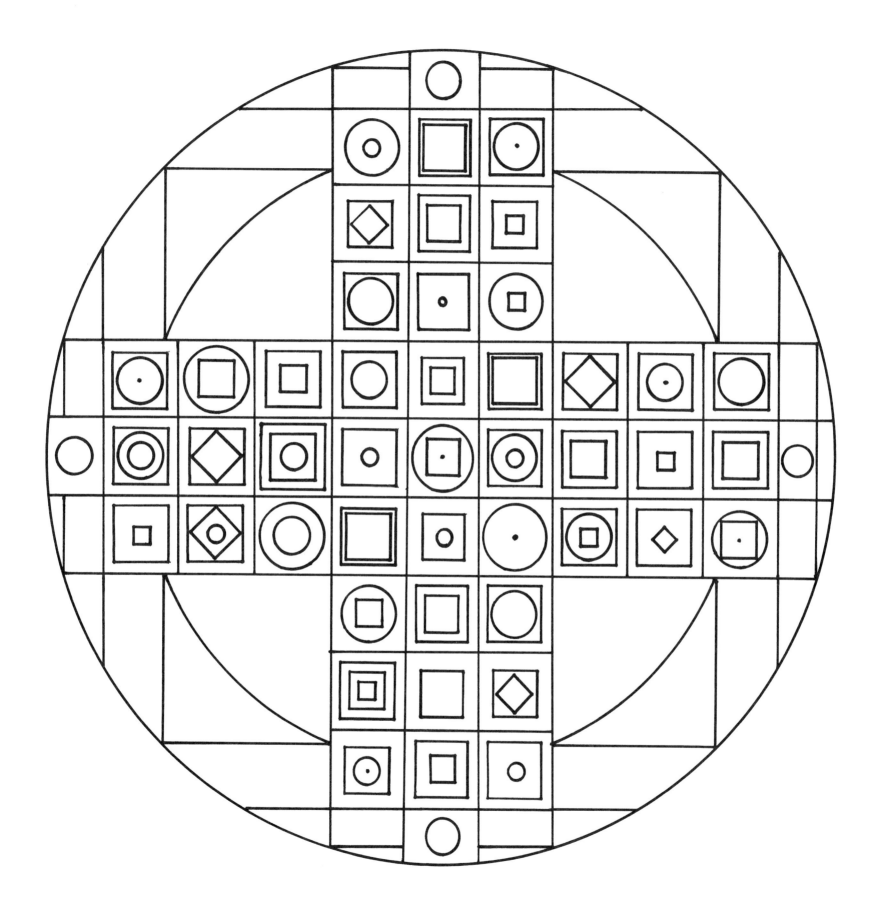

MANDALA 15

The center pattern of this mandala is a hexagram developed in response to the query, what is the situation surrounding this mandala coloring book? The hexagram is called Progress. *Alfred Huang notes, "Proceeding should be stable, gradual, and steady."*

MANDALA 16

A Crusader's cross marks the center of this mandala. Embarking on a quest is sometimes part of your personal journey as you experience Stage Seven, Squaring the Circle.

MANDALA 17

The optical effect of movement is created by rhythmically layered circles generating an outer mandala boundary. The swirling circular paths converge and cross at the center, suggesting a hidden cross that appears to exert magnetic force. Another exploration of Squaring the Circle.

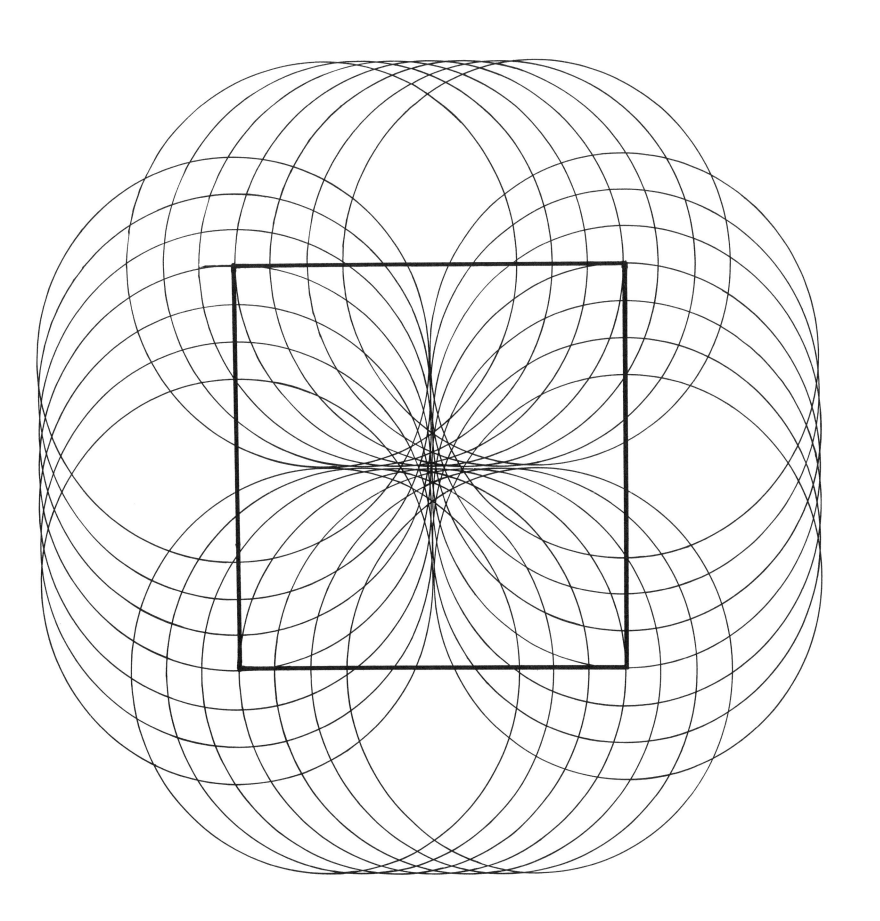

Tendrils unfurl as flowers in full bloom happily show their faces to the sun.

MANDALA 20

A fiery circle encloses the centered Greek cross. Mysterious objects rest on the shoulders of the cross. Use your imagination to decide what they are, and know that it is your unconscious speaking to you.

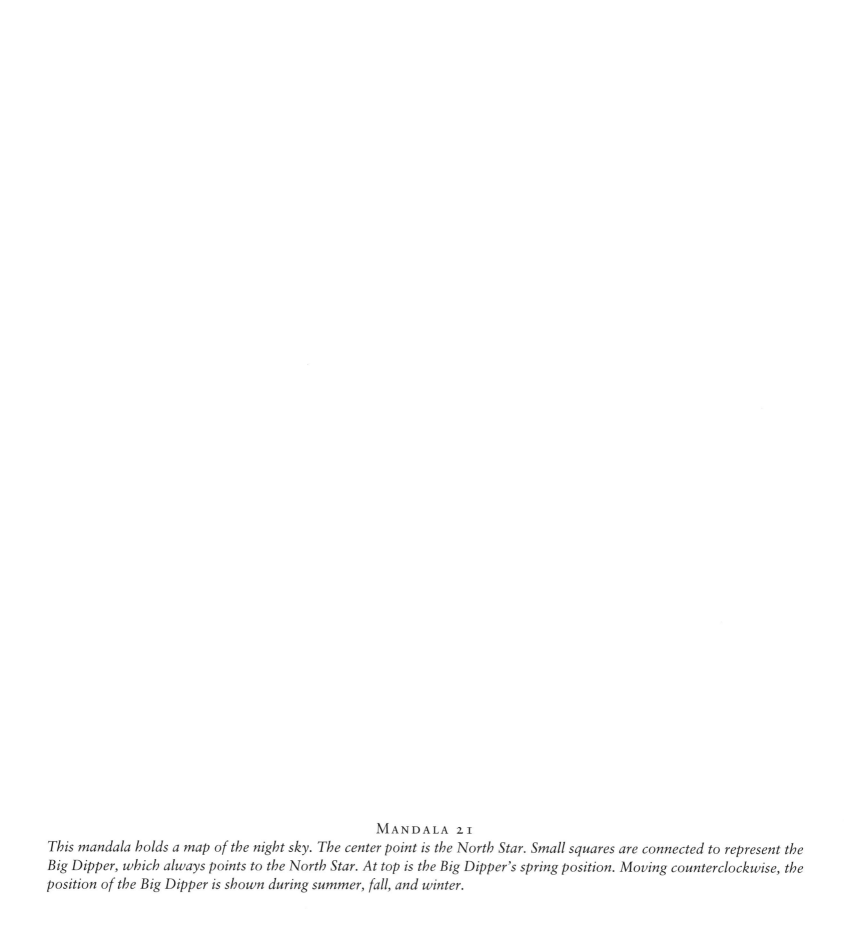

MANDALA 21

This mandala holds a map of the night sky. The center point is the North Star. Small squares are connected to represent the Big Dipper, which always points to the North Star. At top is the Big Dipper's spring position. Moving counterclockwise, the position of the Big Dipper is shown during summer, fall, and winter.

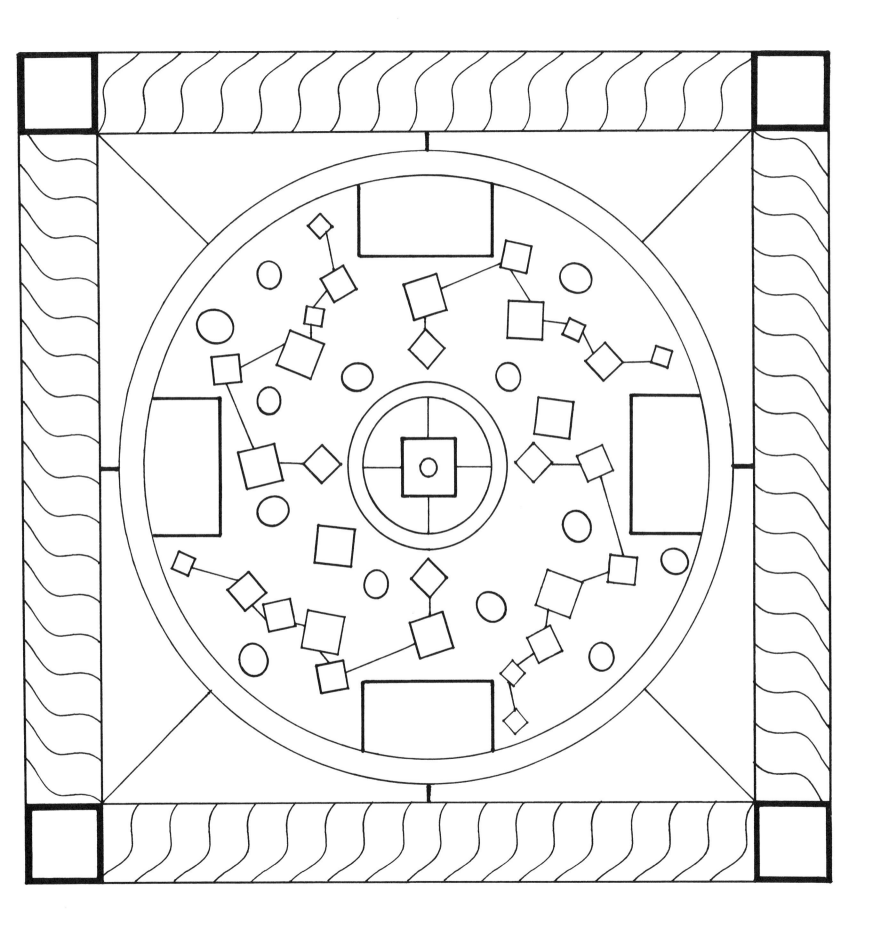

MANDALA 22

The intertwining patterns of Celtic knot work enrich this depiction of a cross that could be carved from stone.

MANDALA 23

Fiddlehead ferns flank the simple cross at the center of this mandala. They suggest the heightened energy that manifests as one moves into Stage Eight, Functioning in the World.

MANDALA 24

This mandala could be a lunar calendar. The smaller circles near the edge of the mandala then would represent the twenty-eight days of a lunar month, or moonth. *The four larger circles could represent the moon and her many phases. Radiance appears to stream outward from the central circle, which in our calendar represents the Sun.*

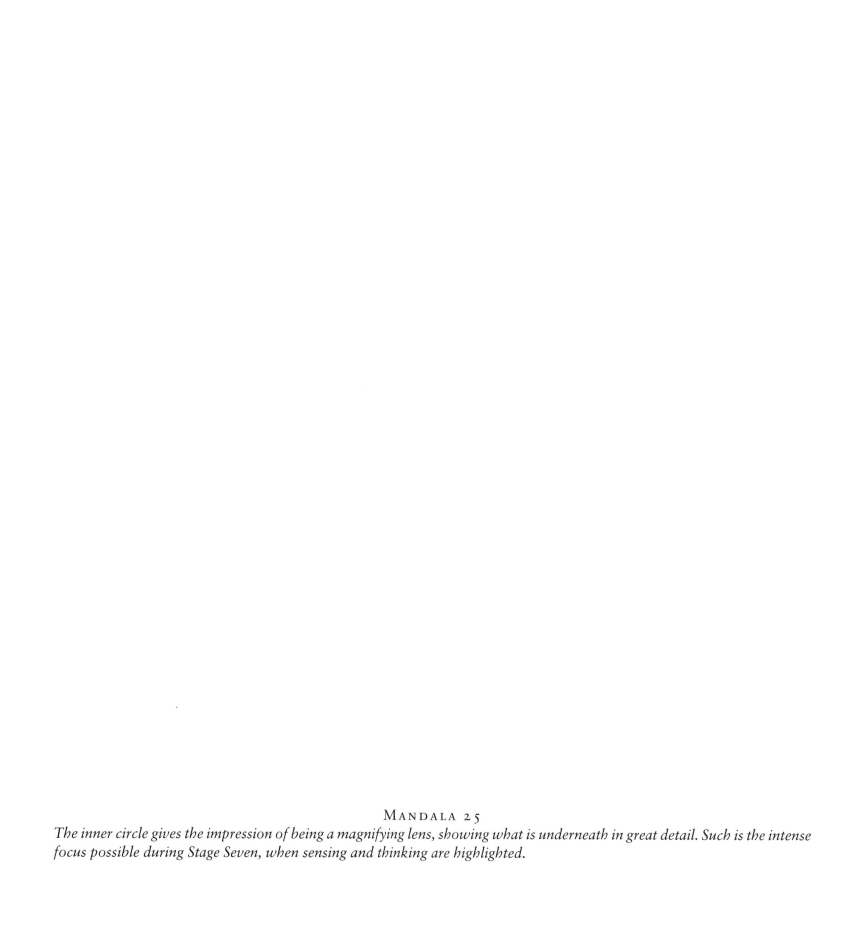

MANDALA 25

The inner circle gives the impression of being a magnifying lens, showing what is underneath in great detail. Such is the intense focus possible during Stage Seven, when sensing and thinking are highlighted.

MANDALA 26

A four-leafed clover grows from the central cross, its leaves mysteriously patterned to suggest—perhaps—bones, pearls, or a warm embrace.

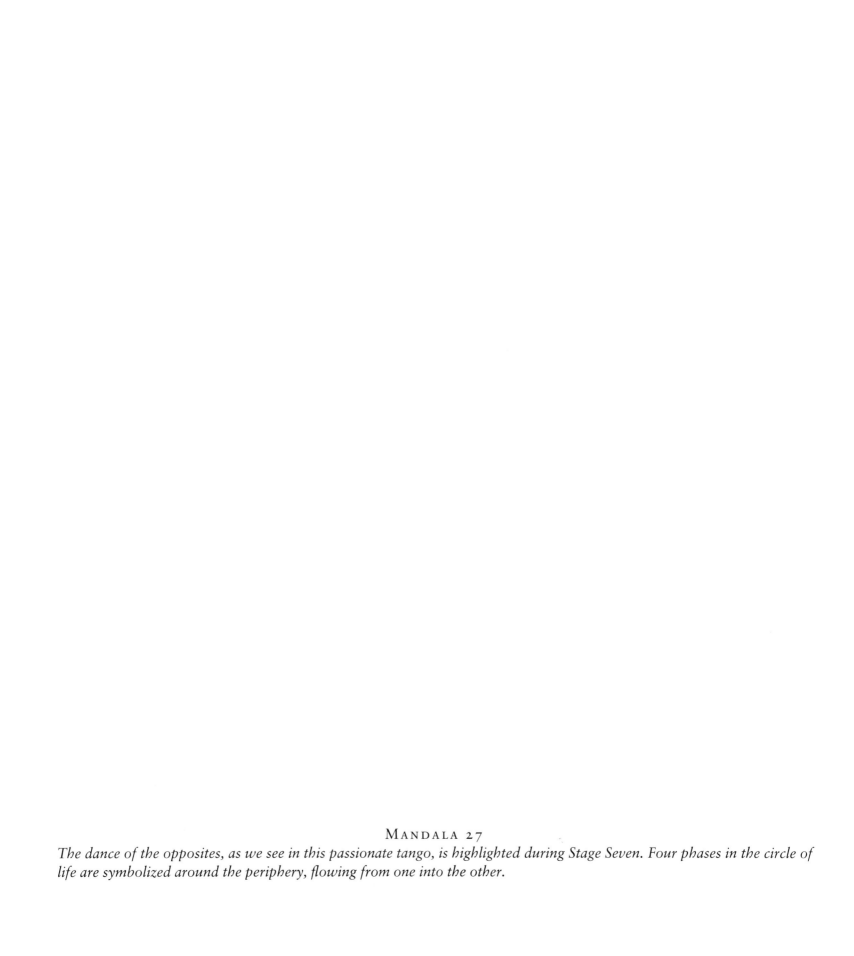

MANDALA 27

The dance of the opposites, as we see in this passionate tango, is highlighted during Stage Seven. Four phases in the circle of life are symbolized around the periphery, flowing from one into the other.

MANDALA 28
Five flowers bring the energy of Stage Eight doing *into a mandala with four tropical plants quietly spreading their leaves.*

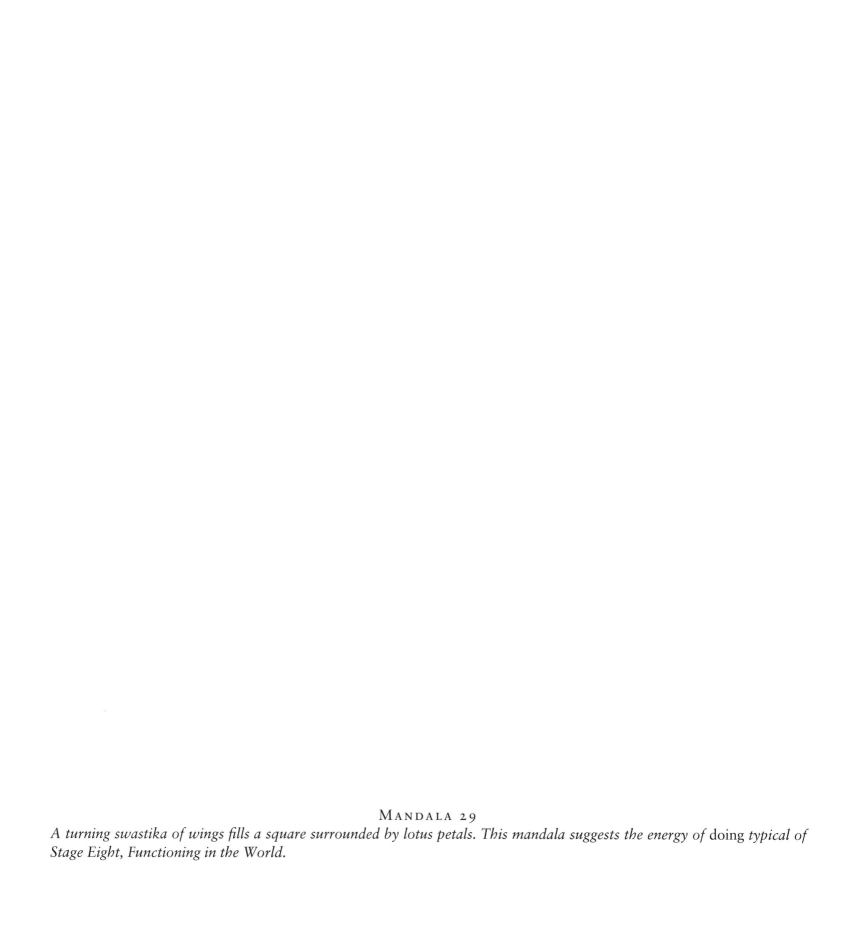

MANDALA 29

A turning swastika of wings fills a square surrounded by lotus petals. This mandala suggests the energy of doing *typical of Stage Eight, Functioning in the World.*

MANDALA 31

Ruffled petals create a many-layered flower that recalls the five points of the human body: head, arms and hands, legs and feet.

MANDALA 32

A commanding star comes forward in this mandala. Vignettes from the cycle of change exemplified in the phases of the moon are shown around the periphery.

MANDALA 33

Stage Eight, Functioning in the World, is a time of working skillfully with people, as suggested by the hand touching five smaller mandalas inside the large circle.

MANDALA 34

The central star anchors circles that seem to spin with centrifugal force into varied configurations. This mandala is a lively depiction of the energy of doing.

MANDALA 35
This mandala appears to celebrate the expanding energy generated by the stage called Functioning in the World.

MANDALA 36

Rotating arms extending from a sturdy square appear to scoop in energy. Coloring this mandala perhaps will increase your energy for doing.

MANDALA 37

Stage Eight is a time when you stand firm and stretch out to touch and shape the world, undaunted by complexity.

MANDALA 38

Stage Eight invites the full expression of your talents, knowledge, and skills. You are the star of your own creations.

Mandala 39

This mandala appears a bit out of balance at first, but take another look. Five air-filled sails turn above a serene structure of four stylized petals. The layers are firmly attached to the center. This whimsical, yet grounded, mandala combines elements of both being *and* doing.

MANDALA 40

A soft flower with five petals is contained and protected by a rainbow band and hexagrams revealing opposite pairings of yin (receptive) energy and yang (active) energy.

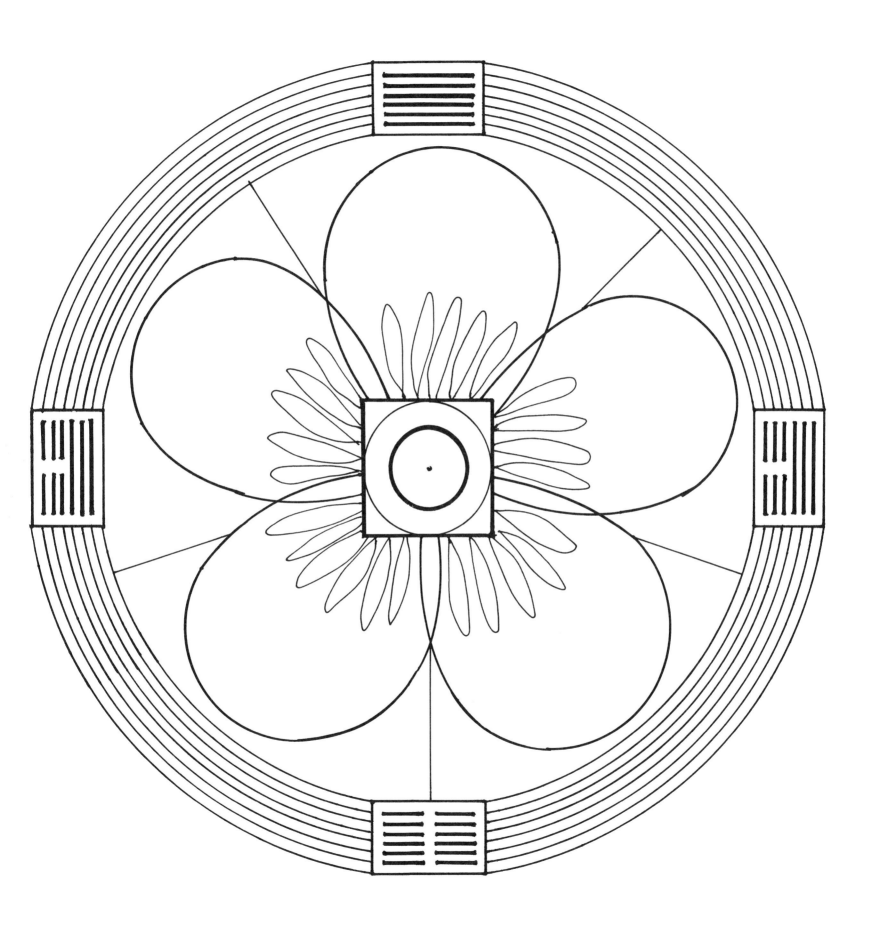

MANDALA 41

This is a lively design with a rotating cross at the center. Four gateways near the boundary of the mandala could symbolize the four cardinal directions, spiritual guides, or aspects of a project you are doing.

MANDALA 42

This design is inspired by traditional Eastern mandalas structured like a temple with four gates. The square recalls Stage Seven, Squaring the Circle, and being. The inner structure of five circles recalls Stage Eight, Functioning in the World, typified by active doing. Multiple lines flow through the mandala suggesting, perhaps, your varied experiences coloring the mandalas of the Great Round included in this book.

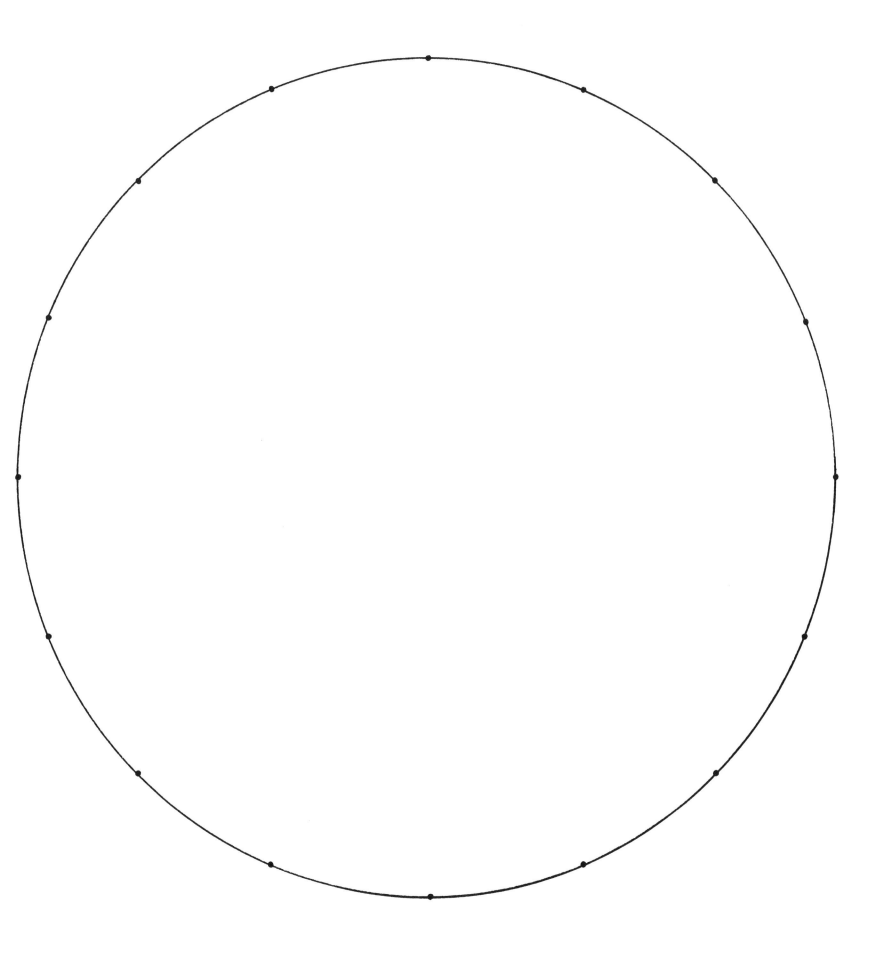

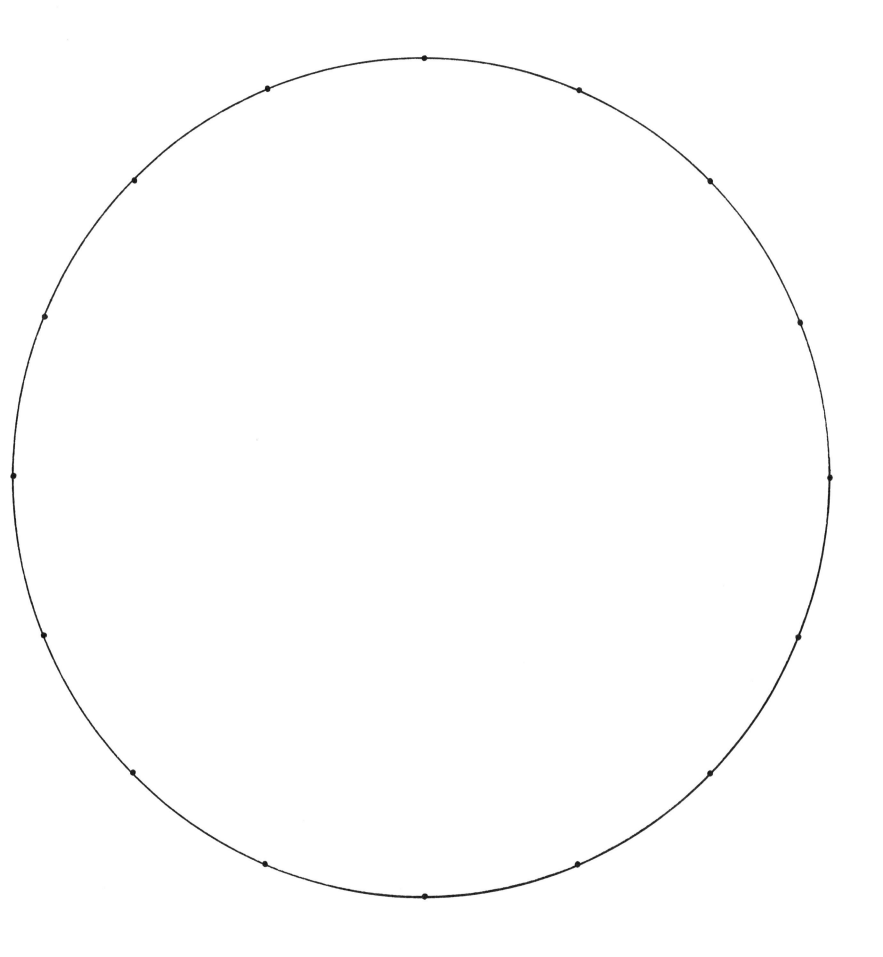

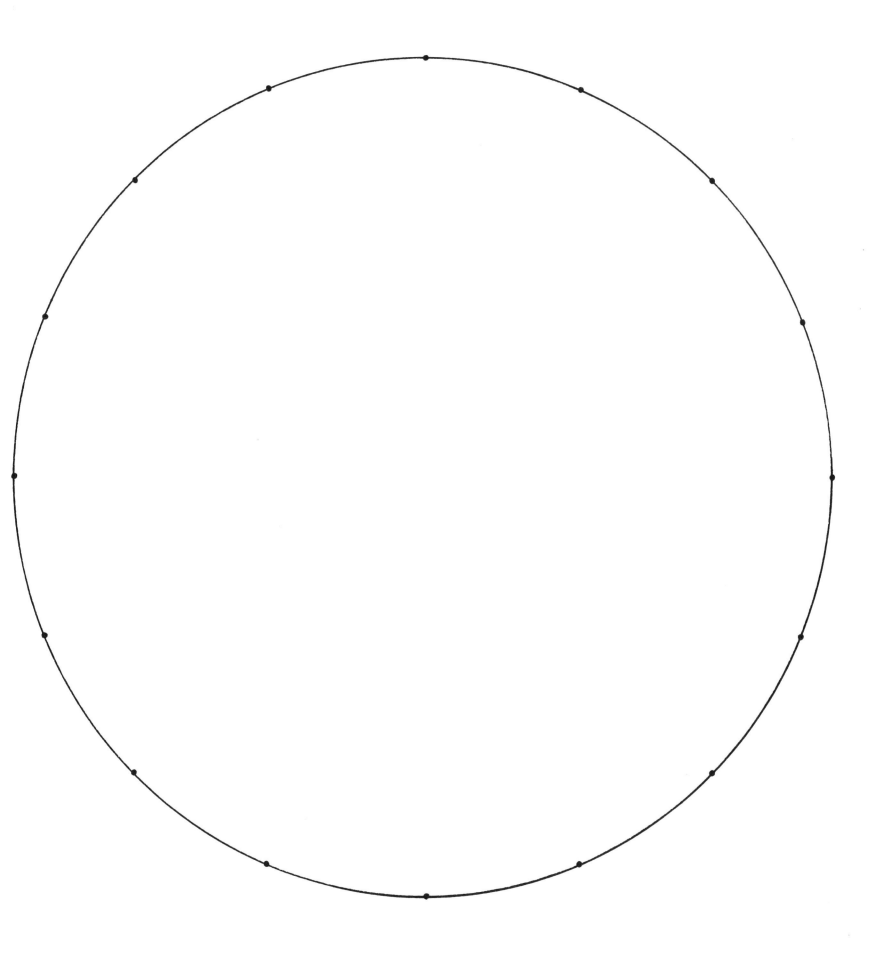